D1573188

All the best,

Roy Romanow,

Premier

2000.

# I Heard the Drums

## Allen Sapp

Stoddart

Toronto • Buffalo

Copyright © Allen Sapp 1996

All rights reserved. No part of this publication may be reproduced or transmitted in any
form or by any means, electronic or mechanical, including photocopying, recording, or
any information storage and retrieval system, without permission in writing from the publisher.

Published in 1996 by Stoddart Publishing Co. Limited

*Distributed in Canada by*
General Distribution Services Inc.
30 Lesmill Road
Toronto, Canada M3B 2T6
Tel. (416) 445-3333
Fax (416) 445-5967
e-mail Customer.Service@ccmailgw.genpub.com

*Distributed in the United States by*
General Distribution Services Inc.
85 River Rock Drive, Suite 202
Buffalo, New York 14207
Toll free 1-800-805-1083
Fax (416) 445-5967
e-mail Customer.Service@ccmailgw.genpub.com

**Cataloguing in Publication Data**
Sapp, Allen, 1929–
    I heard the drums

ISBN 0-7737-2974-7

1. Sapp, Allen, 1929–      2. Cree Indians in art.    3. Indians of North America –
Saskatchewan – Pictorial works.    4. Painters – Saskatchewan – Biography.    I. Title.
ND249.S26A4  1996     759.11     96-930803-5

Cover and Text Design: Tannice Goddard
Transparencies: Patricia Holdsworth, Don Hall (i, 25, 26, 79, 81)

Printed and bound in Hong Kong by Book Art Inc., Toronto.

Opening paintings:
(p i) TRADITIONAL POWWOW, *1991, acrylic on canvas, 121.92 cm x 121.92 cm (48" x 48"), Allen Sapp;*
(p ii) HE'S DRUMMING THE BABY TO SLEEP, *1991, acrylic on canvas, 40.64 cm x 50.80 cm (16" x 20"), Allen Sapp;*
(p vi) HEATING THE DRUMS TO START ROUND DANCE, *1996, acrylic on canvas, 60.96 cm x 60.96 cm (24" x 24"),
Allen Sapp.*

Painting detail on title page: FIVE MEN SINGING, *1996, acrylic on canvas,
55.88 cm x 55.88 cm (22" x 22"), Allen Sapp.*

*In memory of my good friend and manager, James J. Kurtz.*
*Our friendship of twenty years gave me real joy.*
*Our work together took us across Canada and the United States.*
*He treated me like a brother, and for this and*
*many other reasons, I am grateful that the Great Spirit*
*blessed him with a rewarding life.*

# Contents

Allen Sapp

CHIEF POUNDMAKER    1991   *Acrylic on canvas*
*50.80 cm  x 40.64 cm (20" x 16")   Allen Sapp*
Chief Poundmaker was one of our great chiefs and
is still honoured by our people.

# I Heard the Drums

*I* was a very young boy when I first heard the drums. My dad used to play the drums and sing before my brothers and sisters and I went to bed – this made me very happy. He would sing in Cree the songs from Powwows, Round Dances, and Sun Dances.

Our home, on the Red Pheasant Reserve near North Battleford, Saskatchewan, was not very big – there was a wood stove in the kitchen, a table and chairs, and then the place where we slept. Sometimes we would lie in bed and listen to our father play and sing, the drums and his voice lulling us to sleep. Sometimes he would sing in the morning; these songs were usually thanks to Manito for the many good things he had given us. We would all sit around the table, and I can remember my mother being there, but not too much since she died when I was very young.

*Powwow dancers in front of*
*the Allen Sapp Gallery.*

When I was not much older, maybe four years old, my dad took me to a real Powwow at the Little Pine Reserve. I was very excited – we could hear the singing and drumming before we reached the Powwow. As we got closer, the sound of the drums seemed to keep pace with my own heartbeat. My dad lifted me onto his shoulders so I could see over the crowd. The drums looked huge – six or seven men seated around each one, their drumsticks flying high in the air as they pounded out the rhythm.

Then I heard a loud voice calling all the dancers together. There were hundreds of dancers dressed in fancy, colourful costumes. Some of them were only three or four years old and other men and women seemed to be quite old. They were all getting ready for the Grand Entry.

All North American Powwows begin with the Grand Entry. Native veterans carry in the American and Canadian flags (and in Canada sometimes the Union Jack, probably going back to the time when the Treaties were made by the Queen with the native people) and some honoured natives carry the Eagle Staff. Following the flag bearers are many white and native dignitaries, and then come the dancers: the Traditional Dancers (of which I am one), the Fancy Dancers (who dance much faster than the Traditional Dancers), then many others, including the older people and the very young. Once the Grand Entry has been completed, the whole assembly pauses for prayers, led by an Elder in Cree and English. The Powwow is an occasion for spirituality, offering prayers of praise and thanksgiving, and also one of joy, with continuous singing, drumming, and dancing.

Sitting on my father's shoulders, taking in so many different sights and sounds, I didn't realize then how important the Powwow would be in my future. Meeting with friends, dancing with the other dancers, listening to the drums – I always return from them feeling renewed and refreshed, ready to paint.

I also love attending the Round Dances and Sun Dances. Round Dances are usually held in the winter time in homes or other smaller places. There are special Round Dance songs, which are accompanied by the drums, and all of the people join hands in a circle and dance. Sun Dances are sacred to my people. At the Sun Dance, prayers are said for all people and vows made to Manito, the Great Spirit. Those participating will fast for two days and nights, and there is also singing and dancing.

It is hard to understand that in this country where we enjoy so much freedom, there was a time when my people did not enjoy these same freedoms. My dad told me that Sun Dances were outlawed by the Canadian government in 1885. My people continued to hold them secretly until they were again permitted to hold them, in 1962. Many of my white friends understand and tell me how they would have felt if they were not permitted to get together for their religious celebrations.

The feeling of friendship and happiness at the Powwows and dances carries over to my everyday life. I like to think of the happy things in life – some people call it positive thinking. I cannot completely forget some of the unpleasant happenings, and how my parents and grandparents had to overcome many obstacles. But I prefer to remember in my paintings the happier days of my childhood, growing up on the reserve.

Photograph: Daniele Pellegrini

*Allen Sapp in his dancing costume.*

*Allen Sapp's grandmother
(Nokum) Maggie Soonias.*

I was born at the Red Pheasant Reserve on January 2, 1928, in my grandparents' log cabin. My mother was assisted by my grandmother and gave birth to me on the floor of the log cabin. My birth took place in the middle of winter, which is maybe why I enjoy painting winter scenes so much. The winter is a time of year when the land seems so peaceful and quiet. Nature is at rest, the snow blankets the earth, and many animals and trees are sleeping.

I was lucky: I was born into a loving family, whose roots gave me a strong sense of identity. Many people spend their whole lives searching for their beginning, searching for a connection to their family. I know where I came from and for many years I have known where I am going. But this wasn't just a stroke of luck – it began with the love and support of my family and my beloved grandmother, my Nokum.

My mother and dad lived very close to my grandparents. They had seven children, but only Simon, Stella, and I lived to become adults. My mother died when she was very young, and my Nokum raised me. I was very close to my Nokum and to this day she has had a great influence on my life. My people have always believed that the family is not limited to your father and mother – the grandparents were always around to help raise the children.

My grandfather Alfred Soonias had a successful farm with over one hundred head of cattle. We also had many chickens, and I would help my Nokum by gathering eggs in the chicken house. The chickens did not always like me taking away their eggs and sometimes pecked at my hands. I also worked in the garden, planting potatoes and other vegetables. We would go to the store at Cando for flour and sugar, but most of our food we would provide ourselves.

Growing up on the Red Pheasant Reserve helped me to appreciate nature and also hard work. We used horses to plant the crops and to cut hay for the cattle. I would work alongside my dad and my grandfather, and they would show me what to do. It didn't take long before I knew how to harness up the team of horses and get them ready to work. I loved horses – riding them and taking care of them. I decided that I wanted to be a cowboy when I grew up.

We harnessed the horses up to a wagon when we were going into the bush to cut some wood. A good team of horses working together could pull a big load of wood. But this would become impossible if one of the horses decided to go sideways or in a different direction. (I think the same applies to people:

*Maggie Soonias (Allen's grandmother) and her brother Isaac Wuttunee.*

*Left to right: Alex Sapp (Allen's father),*
*Stella Sapp (Allen's sister), and Albert*
*Soonias (Allen's grandfather).*

if we are working together, pulling together, we can accomplish a lot of things. If we go in different directions, we wind up going nowhere.) When the work was done, I helped feed the horses, making sure they had water to drink, and then put them in the barn for the night.

Early in the fall, it was time to harvest the crops. We used to cut the grass with a mower whose long knives had to be sharpened from time to time. We had a stone wheel that could be turned by hand, and an old rubber tire at the bottom of the wooden box supplied water as the wheel turned. I soon learned how to make stooks (stacks of hay), which was hard work. When it was hot I would sometimes lie down in the shade. During threshing time, people would chip in and help their neighbours. Ten or twelve people would come over, and we used to eat outside on a big table. The women prepared the meals — usually meat and potatoes. Sometimes it was deer meat; other times it was beef from our own cows, or chicken.

My dad and grandfather sometimes also worked for other farmers if their own work was done. There was a strong sense of community at the reserve. When we butchered a cow or a deer, everyone helped. The hide would be scraped and stretched, and later used for making moccasins and other items out of the leather. My Nokum was very good at making moccasins and doing beadwork and she showed me how to do this work. The deer meat would be made into pemmican — we would add sugar and rub it into the meat. Sometimes we would rub in mash made with wild berries. The meat would then be stored for the winter.

Even though we had many cows, my grandfather and father would often go out hunting for deer. There were many animals around the reserve at this time. Sometimes they would take me along. Once, after my father shot a deer from his horse, he fell to the ground. He got back up and was happy to see that he got the deer.

Winter was the time when we would work outside cutting wood. We would keep enough wood for ourselves to last through the season and earn some extra money by selling to a white person. This we could do without getting permission from the Indian agent. But we would have to get permission from the agent to sell crops or cattle. The white men could sell whenever they wanted to.

Sometimes we could have received a better price for our crops or cattle when we were ready to sell, but we had to wait for permission. This could very well be why so many Indians who farmed success-fully eventually failed: they did not enjoy the same freedom as their white neighbours. Here we were living on land that our ancestors had inhabited for years and years, and after we negotiated treaties with the representatives of the Queen guaranteeing our freedom, we were denied those freedoms.

During my early years I was not a particularly healthy boy. When I was about eight years old I became very sick and my grandmother's sister said that unless I got a new name – an Indian name – I would die. This was to be the first of many spiritual experiences, although at the time I was too sick to be aware of what was happening. My Nokum told me later that the Nootoka (my grandmother's sister)

*Left to right: Melvin and John Sapp (Allen's nephews), Alex Sapp (Allen's father), and Allen Sapp.*

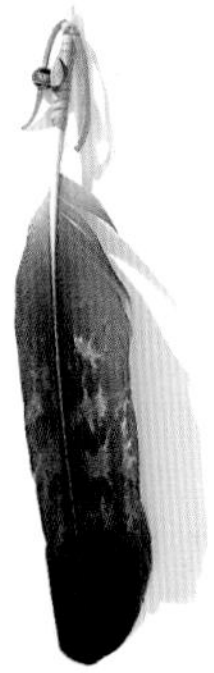

stood by me and placed her hand on my head. In a loud voice, she said, "Your name shall be Kiskayetum"; translated, this means "He perceives it." After this was done she said I would live long and prosperously. I am thankful to Manito that these predictions have come true. As I grew older my health improved and my paintings were the key to earning a good living.

But first, there was yet another illness to get over. When I was about fourteen I was stricken with meningitis and was bedridden. My schooling was interrupted, which at the time didn't seem that important to me. My Nokum was also a medicine woman who knew a lot about Indian medicine. I was nursed back to health by her kindness and loving care as well by her knowledge of medicine and herbs.

Living on the reserve, we did not have many distractions. We did not have much to do with white people except when we went to town to haul some wood or sell some chickens or eggs. This was both good and bad. We were not exposed to all of the temptations of white society, but at the same time we didn't have much opportunity to learn the English language. At home we always spoke in Cree, so it was also difficult for my dad to learn English. He tried to learn, but he was embarrassed to speak it, because some people made fun of him. Since then I have always felt that people shouldn't laugh at other people's faults or make fun of them – they should laugh at themselves.

I spent a couple of years at the Anglican Residential School at Onion Lake. My father took me there, and when he left, I was a little scared, but mostly lonesome. There were about sixty of us there, all Indian, but it was not a very happy experience. No one ever abused me physically or sexually but the way we were disciplined was not like home. We were forbidden to speak Cree – the teachers and everyone connected to the school spoke English – but Cree was the only language I knew. If we were caught speaking Cree to one another we would be punished.

One particular day I was caught speaking Cree to one of my classmates and told that I would have to go up and remain in my room. That afternoon there was a cowboy movie showing in town and I so wanted to go to that movie. I sat in my room and cried.

I look back at the days I spent at the Onion Lake School, and wonder – maybe if the teachers had been more understanding, perhaps if they had been able to speak Cree, it may not have been so difficult for us to learn English. It was almost as if the teachers expected us to speak and write English as well as the white children. They forgot that we had been living on the reserve, isolated from white people. My father and mother, my grandfather and grandmother, they all spoke Cree. Why should we be punished for speaking the language we were brought up in?

I started drawing when I was quite young – around five or six. I would draw with pencils on anything I could find – wrapping paper, cardboard. My Nokum encouraged me. One time I asked her if I could draw her. She said, sure, go ahead. So I did and she was very pleased with the finished drawing. She told me, "Keep on drawing – some day you will be very famous. Keep away from alcohol and things will work out for you." Since then my grandmother has been a favourite subject for many paintings. She was a tall lady, with a strong voice, but a very gentle nature. I can still see her as if she were beside me now when I am painting.

When I first began painting I used a lot of white and black paint – maybe because it was hard to get supplies and these two colours were most readily available. Some of my early paintings were almost like drawings; I used the brush to do some of the things I had taught myself to do by pencil. The winter scenes in

*Allen Sapp painting at
the Assiniboia Gallery.*

these first paintings were often done in shades of black, white, or brown. By mixing the colours I would get different tones of brown and grey. The early summer scenes were often done with a mixture of green and brown. Now I use primary colours in my painting but am able to get many different shades of light and dark colours by mixing the paints until I get just the shade I want.

As I became an adult, I painted full time. Those early days of drawing and painting were very difficult. I would get a small amount of money when someone would give me a picture and ask me to copy it – perhaps a mountain scene with a moose standing by the water. (At that time, I had never been to the mountains.) But I received encouragement and often supplies from Eileen Berryman, who ran a hobby shop in North Battleford. I will never forget her kindness and friendship.

When I was in my mid-thirties, Eileen told me that there was a doctor who wanted to meet me, and who might be interested in my paintings. At that time I had been living on welfare for a few years, both on and off the reserve. The story has been told many times how I travelled by mistake to Saskatoon to see this doctor, only to learn that he lived right here in North Battleford. It did not take long before Dr. Allan Gonor became my very good friend and patron. He was very interested in my paintings, and encouraged me to go off welfare. He guaranteed me a certain amount of money each month, so I wouldn't have to worry about it.

Dr. Gonor arranged with Wynona Mulcaster, an art professor at the University of Saskatchewan in Saskatoon, to meet with us every Saturday for over a year. Although I could not understand English very well at the time, I had that gift of observation and would watch while she demonstrated certain painting techniques and the use of colours. I would then go home and paint pictures, which I would bring along on our next trip to Saskatoon. She encouraged me to paint the way I saw and remembered life on the reserve.

Wynona Mulcaster, together with Dr. Gonor, put on a show of my works in the garden of her home in the summer of 1968. This, my first show, was very success-ful – all of my paintings sold. Wynona was then instru-mental in arranging a show at the Mendel Gallery in Saskatoon; a total of 13,000 people attended. I have learned through life that no one succeeds by them-selves; we all need friends. (I was very happy to be invited when Wynona Mulcaster received the Saskatchewan Arts Board Award in 1993 – and pleased to join her in receiving the Award in 1996.)

More exciting things were to come rather quickly. In 1970, Dr. Gonor arranged for his friend Bill Baker to become my business manager (he was my manager until he died in 1986). After my first show, he and Dr. Gonor arranged other exhibitions, including one in New York. I had never travelled very much out of the immediate vicinity of the Red Pheasant Reserve or North Battleford. Suddenly I was in

*Allen Sapp at the SIFC Powwow in Regina with members of the R.C.M.P. and Regina City Police.*

*Allen Sapp standing in front
of the Allen Sapp Gallery –
The Gonor Collection.*

New York. I was overwhelmed by such a big city. I had never seen buildings so tall and so many people in one place. I stayed at some fancy hotel, and, in truth, I would have been more comfortable sleeping on the floor than in the nice bed.

In our culture we believe that Manito bestows special talents on people and these gifts are to be used for the benefit of all people. Looking back I realize that I was very fortunate in moving ahead so fast. Exhibitions in New York, London, Los Angeles, Montreal, Calgary, Toronto – it all seemed like a dream. This was made possible by the talent that Manito gave me, but also by the many friends who helped me on the way.

When I started to paint life as I remembered it on the reserve, I didn't need any pictures to remind me. It was as if my mind was a camera and would place before me pictures of places and events of many years ago while growing up on the Red Pheasant Reserve. Dr. Gonor often said I had a "photographic memory," and this description has stuck with me ever since.

Both Dr. Gonor and his wife Ruth treated me as if I were part of their family. I like painting at night, since I need the peace and quiet, and many times when I finished some paintings I would take them over to the Gonors. Sometimes it would be eleven or twelve o'clock, and they would be sleeping. But Ruth Gonor would get up and invite me in, take the paintings, which Dr. Gonor would later photograph and number, and usually offer me some tea and apple pie. She was very gracious, even though the hour was very late, and we would have a nice visit.

It was Dr. Gonor's wish that a permanent home be found for my paintings, and after his death in 1986 Ruth Gonor was instrumental in donating over eighty paintings that were to be housed in the Allen Sapp Gallery – the Gonor Collection in North Battleford. I have since been able to donate over thirty paintings to the Gallery and it has become a living memorial to Dr. Gonor, and, I like to think, not just to myself – but to my people, the Cree.

In November 1993, Wayne Rostad from the CBC program *On the Road Again* came to North Battleford to film my life as a painter. We visited the reserve and my grandmother's grave and the place where my log cabin had stood. We walked along in the bush, crunching on the thin blanket of snow that was on the ground that year. The reserve is quite different now and all I could do is point out and describe the way things were when I was a boy growing up a long time ago.

The cabin is no longer there but I can still see everything in my mind as if it were yesterday. The old wooden stove, the calendar hanging on the wall with sweetgrass over it, Nokum sitting on the bed saying her prayers, Nokum sitting doing beads. Come to think of it, I can't remember too much about my Nokum ever scolding me or giving me a spanking. I don't think it was because I was always such a good boy but it must have been that she was such a wonderful Nokum. Some of my earlier paintings of life inside the cabin may have been a little dark,

*Wayne Rostad, host of* On the Road Again, *getting some pointers on playing the drum from Allen Sapp.*

*Allen Sapp and other native artists at the Moscow Exhibition held at the Department of Foreign Affairs and International Trade, Ottawa, on January 31, 1995.*

but you will have to remember that we had no electricity at that time – the only light was from a coal oil lamp, which you often see in my paintings.

When the camera crew and I got back to the Allen Sapp Gallery they wanted me to paint. I sat for a long time. A bare canvas was placed on the easel, with the brushes and paint beside me. Maybe I was a little nervous – the bright lights and the cameras were pointing right at me. I just didn't feel like painting so we went for supper. After supper my present manager, John Kurtz, said to me, "Allen, you promised that the CBC would be able to film you painting. The producer of the program said that she had never had a show cancelled, but if you don't paint it's no go."

So I sat down and started painting. It was a familiar scene – in my mind I could see two teams of horses, with the men cutting wood in the bush. The next day I finished the painting: "Two Men Getting Wood in the Bush." The camera caught me painting from start to finish. I even enjoyed seeing myself paint, and seeing the final picture, when the program was aired on national television in January 1994.

I have been very fortunate that both commercial and public galleries have been good to me. The commercial galleries were behind me right from the beginning. Among public galleries, the Mendel Gallery in Saskatoon was one of my first supporters and has continued to be to this day. When the book *A Cree Life: The Art of Allen Sapp* by John Anson Warner and Thecla Bradshaw came out in 1977, the Mendel Gallery organized an exhibition of my paintings, but they could not interest the Mackenzie Art Gallery in Regina in the exhibition. The

Assiniboia Gallery, owned by the Kurtz family – John, his wife, Monica, and their son James – was then asked to have the exhibition and this was my first meeting with them. The exhibition, which was very successful, was the beginning of a friendship and relationship that has also continued to this day. Almost twenty years after the Mackenzie Art Gallery refused my exhibition, they organized a retrospective exhibition that opened in Regina in 1994 to record crowds and is travelling to other parts of Canada until 1997. (I understand that there were different directors at the Mackenzie Gallery in 1976 and 1994.)

Among the commercial galleries I met many kind, important, and influential people: the Molson family in Montreal who owned the Continental Gallery, the Lourie brothers, Bill and George, who ran the Lourie Gallery in the Royal York Hotel, Toronto. Bill had been with the T. Eaton Company Gallery in Toronto when I had my first show there. I could mention many more friends in galleries in Vancouver, Victoria, Edmonton, Calgary, Kelowna, Banff, Regina, Saskatoon, North Battleford, Winnipeg, Toronto, Hamilton, Kitchener, Ottawa, Montreal, Los Angeles, and New York. Having exhibitions at so many galleries, particularly the galleries in Canada, makes me appreciate what a great country we have. Whenever we had an exhibition of paintings, whether it was in Montreal or Vancouver, it didn't seem to matter that I was an Indian; my art was always appreciated and I was shown many kindnesses. It made me feel good to know that we had such a great country like Canada where even a poor Indian from the Red Pheasant Reserve could make it to the top.

*Allen Sapp visiting the Gessner farm on the outskirts of North Battleford.*

As time has gone on, many honours have come my way because of my painting. I like to think that these honours are not just for me but for all my people. Over the years I have met royalty, prime ministers (Pierre Trudeau invited me to lunch, the next time I was in Montreal), premiers, governor generals, lieutenant governors, judges (fortunately out of court), and many other people. But I am also pleased when some young Indian boy or girl comes up to me at a Powwow or else-where and says, "Hello, Mr. Sapp," and shakes my hand.

Sometimes I wonder: Do people treat me with respect and give me lots of attention because I am an artist or because I am an Indian? I like to think that it is a bit of both. For many years it seems that people thought Indians could only paint in a certain way and were obviously inferior to white artists unless they stuck to "traditional" Indian art. When my paintings began to be accepted by the public there was a little confusion. The experts didn't know how to catego-rize my art. People often compare my work with that of other artists. Some people say that although I am Indian I don't paint like an Indian. This seems rather strange as many native people paint in different styles. A friend of Dr. Gonor, the famous historian Will Durant, thought that I painted like a European. (At the time, I had not been very far away from the Red Pheasant Reserve, let alone to Europe.) I say that I paint as I remember the world before me – the land, the horses, the beauty of the seasons (especially the winter, which is with us for such a long time on the prairies that you either learn to live with it or leave it). Then some of my friends felt that success came too quickly for me. Why does Allen Sapp get all of the attention, they wondered. Why not us? On the whole, most people were very supportive, both white and Indian, encouraging me and sharing in my happiness.

Although I paint life like I remember it on the reserve as I was growing up, in many ways it was not too different from other farm families'. At different shows white people will come up to me and say, "My father did the same things that you are showing in your painting, 'Cutting Wood in the Winter.'" They see the cows in the pasture and it reminds them that as a young man or woman they also looked after the cows. And many Cree men and women will come up to me with tears in their eyes as they see certain paintings describing scenes as I remembered them on the reserve. Paintings of drummers and dancers at Powwows are important to record our culture and history and a lot of the time I want to make sure that every detail shows upon the costumes of the dancers – everything has to be correct.

When I sit down at my canvas to start a painting I will usually have a good idea – you might say I have a good picture in my own mind as to what the painting will be like. If I am going to paint a picture of my Nokum feeding the chickens, everything is very clear. The chicken house is not too far from our log cabin. The chickens start to come

Photograph: Don Hall

*Allen Sapp drumming for a Round Dance during
the* Kiskayetum – Allen Sapp: A Retrospective
*exhibit at the MacKenzie Art Gallery.*

running as they see Nokum approaching. They know that she is going to have something for them to eat. Nokum likes her chickens and that is why the painting always looks cheerful and happy. Usually the painting will have a blue sky. This doesn't mean that Nokum wouldn't feed the chickens on a day when the sky was grey; I just always seem to want to paint her with a blue sky.

When I paint a sunset or sunrise sky the colours just seem to jump out at me. People like these paintings, particularly the winter scenes, and are excited by the prairie sky. One time at a show in Toronto someone remarked that they had never seen a sunset like one shown in my painting. Of course in the big cities you sometimes don't see the sunrise and sunset – all you see are big buildings. On the prairies you can go out in the country and see forever; the horizon seems to never end.

I have always liked painting the sky. At the opening of my retrospective exhibition in North Battleford, Glenn Hornick, mayor of North Battleford, called me over. "Allen, come on outside, I want to show you something. See, there is an Allen Sapp sky." The sun was going down and the sky was a mixture of beautiful red and light yellow. I said, "Only Manito can make a beautiful sky like that, and I am glad that you feel I can paint it."

When I paint a scene of men working in the woods and cutting down some trees, the sky may be grey, blue, or it might be a sunset, for we would be working in all kinds of weather. Sometimes the snow would be falling, or there would be quite a wind and the horses would have to take us home in a blizzard. Anyone who has lived on the prairies knows how dangerous a prairie blizzard can be. In such cases we would be so dependent on our team of horses – they always seemed to be able to get us home in a storm, even if we couldn't see a thing and they were hauling a load of wood. No wonder we were so fond of our horses.

Sometimes people say I have painted too many pictures of people hauling wood in the winter. That may be true, but no one ever said that the Group of Seven artists painted too many landscapes. Cutting and hauling wood was a way of life on the prairies – especially on the reserve where I grew up. My horses were not only good for work, they were also our friends. No wonder I feel good about painting horses – very fine, intelligent animals.

Many people have tried to explain what my paintings are like – how they may resemble a certain style. I have never really had any lessons and consider myself a self-taught artist, though I learned a lot from watching Wynona Mulcaster paint. I like to think that my paintings tell the story of my people in the early days as they worked and lived on the reserve. I have seen books in which other artists – usually white men – would do the same thing. They would paint scenes of what they saw in the West. When I visited the Buffalo Bill Museum in Cody, Wyoming, the Russell Museum in Great Falls, Montana, and the Glenbow Museum in Calgary, I saw many paintings that showed how different artists saw the people, the land, and the animals – Russell and Remington, particularly, whose paintings are western and show a lot of cowboys. My paintings seem different, but do the same thing – show the land on the prairies, the hills in the Battleford area,

Photograph: Don Hall

*Allen Sapp drumming at Family Focus during the* Kiskayetum – Allen Sapp: A Retrospective *exhibit at the MacKenzie Art Gallery.*

*Young student drawing at the Allen Sapp Gallery.*

the people as they lived in their homes on the different reserves surrounding the Battleford area of Saskatchewan.

Sometimes even when unhappy things happen in your life some good can come out of it. When as a child I was lying in bed for a long time sick with meningitis I developed a sense of seeing things in a different light. When I started painting it seemed that I could see things in a different perspective. That is why some of my paintings look as if I were up in a tree looking down, while others give the impression of someone being very small and looking up. I am sure there is some explanation for all of this for those who are learned in the arts, but to me it just seems very real when I paint that way — that's how I see it in my mind.

The Indian way has always been to share one's good fortune with others. I have been happy that I have been able to do this in many ways. Helping with the Indian Summer and Winter games in Saskatchewan in 1994 and 1995 was a rewarding experience. I met old friends and made many new ones. The youngsters participating in the games were really terrific. Whenever I am invited to special events, I feel that I am acting for my Cree people and the honour is for them.

My paintings have been chosen for UNICEF cards for the third time. In 1996 three of my paintings will be used on their Christmas cards, marking UNICEF's fiftieth anniversary. I am pleased to help out in this way as there is so much suffering by children in many parts of the world. Children must be shown love everywhere. And we must not forget children in Canada who also may be in need of love and care.

As I look back at my own childhood, and my development as an artist, I am very concerned that our young people be given help and encouragement so that they will have a good life. I tell them if I can come off a reserve and succeed in becoming a great painter, then every young Indian can do the same – they can have the same dreams and ambitions. Yes, I received a lot of help from people along the way, but nobody could make me paint. I wanted first of all to make my Nokum proud of me – I wanted her prediction to come true. My Nokum died before I became well known as an artist but I know that she is still with me in spirit. My father, who lived to be over ninety years of age, was able to witness my recognition as an artist. I know that he was proud that his son, a Cree Indian from the Red Pheasant Reserve, would do so well.

In the past many Indians were great horsemen and I think that is why there is such an interest in rodeos. My nephew John Sapp was good at chuckwagon races and there are many other Indians who are doing quite well on the rodeo circuit, including Edgar Baptiste from Red Pheasant Reserve. Young people can also be good in sports. Many of my young Indian friends have been playing hockey and doing well. Even today in my own province young Indian boys have to put up with some bad name calling when they are playing hockey. I tell them, "You can't let it bother you. You can show people that you are as good as anyone and it doesn't matter what race you are." I have met some fine Indian hockey players and I am happy that an Indian, Ted Nolan, is now the coach of a professional hockey team – the Buffalo Sabres.

Indians can succeed in every area of life – not just in sports. My good friend Gordon Tootoosis of the Red Pheasant Reserve is an

*Allen Sapp watching young students doing some sidewalk painting in front of the Allen Sapp Gallery.*

outstanding actor and has appeared in many television shows and movies. When he comes back to the reserve he is only too happy to spend time with young children, urging them to get ahead in life.

Some people ask why the Indian should get so much attention or special treatment. My answer is that we don't want to be treated differently, just equally.

I visit the Allen Sapp Gallery almost every day and Dean Bauche, the Curator of the Gallery, often calls me when there are classes of school children attending. Dean has arranged an educational program: when the students visit the Gallery they not only see my paintings and learn about them, but they are also exposed to stories on art. If I am asked, I will speak to the children, play the drums, and lead in a Round Dance. These activities not only keep our culture alive with Cree children but also help white children to understand our people.

All my life I have followed my grandmother's advice and never taken alcohol. I don't remember either my father or grandfather drinking. Now when I talk to young people I encourage them to stay away from "stupid things" like alcohol and drugs.

One of the nice things about Powwows and Sun Dances is that no alcohol or drugs are allowed. The dancers, singers, and those who come to watch do not need these evils to make them happy. It would be good if more people were aware that these events are more a part of Indian life and culture than what is so often depicted on television and in movies. People should see more of our culture and spirituality, rather than the violence that is so often shown on the screen. It makes me sad when I see movies like *Dance Me Outside*, which show our young people sitting around drinking beer and fighting. The scenes I saw in that movie were disgusting and portrayed young native people in a very poor light. There were so many closeups of young Indians drinking beer, so vivid that you could read the label – it made me wonder if the movie was sponsored by a brewery. This is not the way life is on most of our reserves. There are many good Indian people living on the reserves, but they never seem to be recognized.

Unfortunately, the same negative and degrading attitude that is displayed towards Indian people by the media is also displayed towards our country. The TV programs and news broadcasts never seem to find anything good to say about our country and always seem to enjoy repeating all of the bad things that happen.

I speak a lot about painting in this book because that is what I have been doing now for thirty years. I have many friends who are also artists – both Indian and white people. I encourage any young people who want to become artists and have the talent to work hard – they can succeed. However, for all of our young Cree friends I have this message. Don't miss the opportunity to have an education. You will be able to learn something which will help you later on in life – to earn a living – and to live a happier life. You have to do this while you are young. I learned to draw and paint when I was just a young boy. This was a gift from Manito, but if I didn't continue painting and try always to do better I would not be where I am today.

*Allen Sapp.*

I like to ask my young friends to listen to the voices of our elders. Many stories have been passed on from generation to generation. Our fathers and mothers would pass on what they knew about our culture, our heritage. We had great respect for them, as we did for our elders. It touches my heart when I hear the elders pray or talk about the old days. This was the Cree way – stories would be passed on from one generation to the next. There was no written Cree language until recently so everything had to be passed on by word of mouth, person to person.

My wish is that more of our young people will hear the drums – if they listen they will hear the voices of our ancestors telling them our glorious past, our culture, and what it means to be an Indian. Knowing our language and culture can make a big difference in their lives. I tell them, don't wait until you are old before you learn to appreciate our culture – if you wait too long it may be too late.

I tell them, you can have a good life and be proud of your heritage if you listen to the drums.

SUN DANCE AT NIGHT  *1969  Pastel on paper  43.18 cm x 59.69 cm (17" x 23.5")  Allen Sapp*
The Sun Dance would go on for two days and nights and seemed to be particularly spiritual
and impressive at night under the moon and the stars.

HAVING SOME TEA   *1992   Acrylic on canvas   152.40 cm x 213.36 cm (60" x 84")   Allen Sapp*
Cutting wood in the bush was hard work and the men would stop working for a while,
make a fire, and have some tea.

SUN DANCE ON THE RESERVE    *1992   Acrylic on canvas   121.92 cm x 182.88 cm (48" x 72")   Allen Sapp*
The Sun Dance is a sacred spiritual experience for Indian people. Prayer is made for all people and
those participating go away feeling renewed and refreshed.

PREPARING FOR THE POWWOW    *1992   Acrylic on canvas   121.92 cm x 182.88 cm (48" x 72")   Allen Sapp*

Before the start of the Powwow the dancers would change into their costumes. Nowadays there are not
too many tipis to change in; they have been replaced by campers and vans.

NOKUM MAKING BANNOCK    *1988   Acrylic on canvas   60.96 cm x 91.44 cm (24" x 36")   Allen Sapp*
Sometimes Nokum would make the bannock outdoors. I can remember how good it smelled
when it was cooking by the fire.

DINNER TIME    *1968   Acrylic on board   45.72 cm x 60.96 cm (18" x 24")   Allen Sapp*

My grandfather had over one hundred head of cattle and so he would also plant oats and make hay.

At harvest time there were extra workers around, and if the weather was good we would enjoy eating outside.

PLANTING POTATOES    *1986   Acrylic on canvas   45.72 cm x 60.96 cm (18" x 24")   Allen Sapp*

A hand plow pulled by a horse would get the ground ready, then I would often help

my Nokum plant potatoes.

DAD GETTING WATER FOR THE HOUSE
*1995   Acrylic on canvas   50.80 cm x 50.80 cm
(20" x 20")   Allen Sapp*
Water for the home was where you found it on the reserve. I remember the beautiful colours in the sky when I would go with my dad to bring some water home.

Allen Sapp

WASHING CLOTHES OUTSIDE    *1995*
*Acrylic on canvas   60.96 cm x 60.96 cm*
*(24" x 24")   Allen Sapp*
People on the reserve liked being outdoors. In
the summertime they would spend as much
time as possible outside doing chores
like washing clothes.

NOKUM MAKING MOCCASINS FOR ME
*1995   Acrylic on canvas   50.80 cm x 50.80 cm*
*(20" x 20")   Allen Sapp*
Nokum was good at a lot of things, including
moccasins. She would use deerhide or cowhide
to make the moccasins and would then include
some fancy beadwork.

LOOKING FOR PRAIRIE CHICKEN  *1995*
*Acrylic on canvas  60.96 cm x 60.96 cm*
*(24" x 24")  Allen Sapp*
Even though we had chickens on the reserve
men would still go out hunting for prairie
chicken. And they could always depend on a
younger member of the family to eagerly go
with them.

My Brother's Wife's Brother    *1971   Acrylic on canvas*
*60.96 cm x 45.72 cm (24" x 18")   Allen Sapp*
I used to draw pictures of people and later on also painted people
that I remembered.

GETTING THE HORSE READY   *1986   Acrylic on canvas   45.72 cm x 60.96 cm (18" x 24")   Allen Sapp*
We were very proud of our horses and so we usually had good harnesses. It would take a little time
to get the horse ready but we enjoyed it.

TWO MEN GETTING WOOD IN THE BUSH *1993 Acrylic on canvas 45.72 cm x 60.96 cm (18" x 24") Allen Sapp*
Men cutting wood in the bush is a very clear picture in my mind. This painting was done while the TV cameras from
*On the Road Again* recorded my every move and stroke on the canvas.

MY GRANDFATHER STRETCHING A WEASEL SKIN   *1993   Acrylic on canvas   40.64 cm x 50.80 cm (16" x 20")   Allen Sapp*
The skins of many animals, including rabbit, weasel, and deer, were used for making clothing or moccasins.
It was important to properly scrape and stretch the skin so that it could be used to make different things.

THE MAN IS SINGING WHILE SHE'S DOING BEADS   *1990*
*Acrylic on canvas  60.96 cm x 45.72 cm (24" x 18")   Allen Sapp*
Singing and playing the drums are often done in the home
and not just at Powwows. Women doing beads find the singing
of Indian songs much better than watching television.

FINISHED COOKING BANNOCK    *1971   Acrylic on canvas  60.96 cm x 45.72 cm (24" x 18")   Allen Sapp*

Nokum was very good at making bannock and would often do it outside in the summertime.

A FAMILY EATING LUNCH    *1991   Acrylic on canvas   40.64 cm x 50.80 cm (16" x 20")   Allen Sapp*
Our home on the reserve was not fancy, but we would have a wood stove and a wooden table
around which we would sit and have our meals.

MOTHER IS SINGING THE BABY TO SLEEP   *1991   Acrylic*
*on canvas   50.80 cm x 40.64 cm (20" x 16")   Allen Sapp*
The baby is in a mossbag, which was used by Indian mothers to
keep their babies snug and warm. The mossbag which was used
when I was a baby is now held by my brother Simon.

CHICKENS ARE SLEEPING *1993 Acrylic on canvas 40.64 cm x 50.80 cm (16" x 20") Allen Sapp*
My Nokum had many chickens and this is how I remember the inside of the chicken house.

I'M HELPING NOKUM FEED THE CHICKENS
*1995   Acrylic on canvas  60.96 cm x 60.96 cm*
*(24" x 24")   Allen Sapp*
I can still see my grandmother feeding the
chickens as if it were yesterday. I loved being
with her when she was feeding them.

THE ANGLICAN CHURCH THE WAY IT USED TO BE   *1994   Acrylic on canvas   60.96 cm x 91.44 cm (24" x 36")   Allen Sapp*
I have painted the Anglican Church on the Red Pheasant Reserve the way I remember it. It is no longer there.

RED PHEASANT SCHOOL A LONG TIME AGO    *1988   Acrylic on canvas   40.64 cm x 50.80 cm (16" x 20")   Allen Sapp*
The old schoolhouse on the Red Pheasant Reserve is also just a memory to me as it is no longer there.

MENDING PANTS FOR HER BOY 1995
*Acrylic on canvas 60.96 cm x 60.96 cm*
*(24" x 24") Allen Sapp*
Some of the things that mothers had to do
on the reserve were not different from those
of mothers in the city. Mending pants was
necessary as there was not too much money
for new clothes.

FATHER WILL BE HOME SOON   *1995*
*Acrylic on canvas   50.80 cm x 50.80 cm*
*(20" x 20")   Allen Sapp*
In the summertime many people on the reserve
lived in tipis. The meals would be cooked
outside on nice days and we would wait for
Dad to return from hunting.

PUTTING THE HORSE IN THE BARN   *1995*
*Acrylic on canvas   60.96 cm x 60.96 cm*
*(24" x 24")   Allen Sapp*
After a hard day's work, my dad would make
sure that the horses were put in the barn and
fed, even before he came into the house for
his meal.

MAKING A SLEIGH FOR A LIL' BOY   1994
*Acrylic on canvas   55.88 cm x 55.88 cm*
*(22" x 22")   Allen Sapp*
When I was a little boy most of our toys were made by my father or grandfather. They made very good sleighs, which we used to slide down hills.

PLAYING HOCKEY AT SUNDOWN *1995*
*Acrylic on canvas 60.96 cm x 60.96 cm*
*(24" x 24") Allen Sapp*
After supper and when the sun was going
down was a good time to play outside. A little
bit of ice behind the house would be all that
was needed for a few children to play hockey.

**TWO LIL' KIDS SLIDING**   *1993   Acrylic on canvas   40.64 cm x 50.80 cm (16" x 20")   Allen Sapp*
This painting has been chosen by UNICEF to be part of the 1996 card series, celebrating
UNICEF's fiftieth anniversary.

GOING TO THE CHRISTMAS CONCERT
*1995   Acrylic on canvas   60.96 cm x 60.96 cm*
*(24" x 24")   Allen Sapp*
It seemed to add to the spirit of the season,
going to the Christmas concert in a
horse-drawn sleigh.

I'M DRAWING AND NOKUM IS DRINKING TEA    *1993   Acrylic
on canvas   50.80 cm x 40.64 cm (20" x 16")   Allen Sapp*
My Nokum always encouraged me to draw and she would sit and watch
me. I would draw on scraps of paper or whatever was around.

THE ROUND DANCE   *1987   Acrylic on canvas   101.60 cm x 152.40 cm (40" x 60")  Allen Sapp*
The Round Dance is usually held indoors in different homes. The drummers will have hand drums
rather than the big drums used at the Powwows.

LIL' FELLOW HOLDING A BALL    *1987   Acrylic on canvas   40.64 cm x 50.80 cm (16" x 20")   Allen Sapp*
Little children must be shown lots of love and attention. Playing ball can be one way to keep them happy.

**THOSE WERE HAPPY TIMES**   *1993   Acrylic on canvas   121.92 cm x 182.88 cm (48" x 72")   Allen Sapp*

Years ago people coming to the Powwows would set up their tipis, which were often quite colourful
and decorated with painted symbols. They would meet old friends and make new ones.

MAKING BEADWORK    *1974   Acrylic on canvas   40.64 cm x 50.80 cm (16" x 20")   Allen Sapp*
Most of the ladies used to be quite good at doing beadwork. I wish more of the young girls would learn
how to do beadwork as it can be beautiful in costumes for dancing and also for moccasins and clothing.

THE RETRIEVER    *1968   Acrylic on canvas   45.72 cm x 60.96 cm (18" x 24")   Allen Sapp*
Hunting was very important and some hunters were fortunate in that they had a good dog
who would go out in the water and bring in the ducks.

HAVING A SWIM    *1980   Acrylic on canvas   40.64 cm x 50.80 cm (16" x 20")   Allen Sapp*
In the wintertime, when there was ice, the children would skate and play hockey. In the
summertime, if there was water around, they would all enjoy having a swim.

HARD PULL    *1968   Oil on canvas board   55.88 cm x 71.12 cm (22" x 28")   Allen Sapp*
The horses had to be strong as sometimes they would have to pull some tree stumps in the bush.

MAN AND HIS DOG    *1970   Acrylic on
canvas   60.96 cm x 45.72 cm (24" x 18")*
*Allen Sapp*
There were always many horses and dogs on
the reserve. These animals were really part of
the family.

HAVING A BATH    *1968   Acrylic on masonite   45.72 cm x 60.96 cm (18" x 24")   Allen Sapp*
Little boys did not mind having a bath when they could be outside in a slough in the summertime.

PULLING A LOG    *1970   Acrylic on canvas   45.72 cm x 60.96 cm (18" x 24")   Allen Sapp*
It is a cold frosty day, the man is dressed warmly, and his dependable horse is ready for
the hard work of pulling a log in the bush.

HELPING DAD CARRY IN THE WOOD
*1994 Acrylic on canvas 50.80 cm x 50.80 cm*
*(20" x 20") Allen Sapp*
On the reserve little children would always like
to be with their mothers and dads, and even
though they could only carry a small load, they
liked to help carry in the wood.

THE WHOLE FAMILY WENT TO GET WATER   *1992   Acrylic on canvas   40.64 cm x 50.80 cm (16" x 20")   Allen Sapp*
Some people had wells on the reserve and everyone in the family would go along to help carry the water home.

BAKING MORE BANNOCK    *1976   Acrylic on canvas   45.72 cm x 60.96 cm (18" x 24")   Allen Sapp*

Some people call bannock "Indian bread" and even today it is a favourite when people

gather at Powwows. Sometimes people will put cinnamon and honey or sugar on it.

LIL' FELLA GOING ON THE TRAIN WITH
HIS GRANDFATHER   *1994   Acrylic on
canvas   60.96 cm x 60.96 cm
(24" x 24")   Allen Sapp*
The memories are still there, but the steam
locomotive and the train have gone the way of
the buffalo. There used to be a train running
through Cando on the Red Pheasant Reserve
but not for many years.

VISITING SOME PEOPLE    *1968   Acrylic on masonite   50.80 cm x 60.96 cm (20" x 24")   Allen Sapp*
When you went to visit some friends they would make you feel right at home. We would talk and
laugh and quite often have supper with them.

THEY WILL BE DRUMMERS SOME DAY
*1995   Acrylic on canvas   60.96 cm x 60.96 cm*
*(24" x 24")   Allen Sapp*
The drummers and singers learn the songs from
someone else — they are passed on from one
to another. That is why it is so important for
young children to listen and learn the songs.

DRYING DEER MEAT    *1972   Acrylic on canvas   60.96 cm x 91.44 cm (24" x 36")   Allen Sapp*
Most of the men living on the reserves were good hunters, so there was always plenty of
deer meat that had to be dried and put away for the winter.

GOING FOR PRAIRIE CHICKEN    *1968   Acrylic on board   60.96 cm x 76.20 cm (24" x 30")   Allen Sapp*
Years ago there seemed to be plenty of prairie chickens on the reserve, and men would usually return
home with one or two birds.

THE FISH TRAP    *1968   Acrylic on canvas   45.70 cm x 60.96 cm (18" x 24")   Allen Sapp*
There were a few lakes not too far from the Red Pheasant Reserve and some of the men
would make a fish trap to catch fish.

FIVE MEN SINGING    *1996   Acrylic on canvas 55.88 cm x 55.88 cm (22" x 22")   Allen Sapp* These five men are singing Round Dance songs at a Round Dance. There are different songs for the Powwows, Sun Dances, and Round Dances, sung in Cree to the beat of the drums.

**AN INDOOR POWWOW** *1995 Acrylic on canvas 45.72 cm x 60.96 cm (18" x 24") Allen Sapp*
Indoor Powwows may be held in small halls or homes and will not have as many dancers, singers,
or drummers as the large outdoor Powwows.

TWO LADIES GOING TO GET SENECA    *1991   Acrylic on canvas   40.64 cm x 50.80 cm (16" x 20")   Allen Sapp*
Seneca grew wild out in the field. The ladies would go out to dig seneca root, which was used in Indian medicine.

NOKUM COMING TO VISIT    *1993   Acrylic on canvas   60.96 cm x 91.44 cm (24" x 36")   Allen Sapp*
This painting has been chosen by UNICEF to be part of the 1996 card series, celebrating
UNICEF's fiftieth anniversary.

CHUCKWAGON RACE    *1993   Acrylic on Canvas   205.74 cm x 266.70 cm (81" x 105")   Allen Sapp*
Indians have always been very good horsemen so it only seems natural that they would like rodeos
and chuckwagon races. Many of these races are held on the reserves and, of course, the goal is to
be in the Calgary Stampede.

GOING HOME WITH A LOAD OF WOOD   *1968   Acrylic on masonite   60.96 cm x 45.72 cm (24" x 18")   Allen Sapp*
After a long day cutting wood in the bush, it felt real good to be going home with a full load.

FIVE MEN STOOKING    *1992   Acrylic on canvas   121.92 cm x 182.88 cm (48" x 72")   Allen Sapp*
Stooking was the way in which we farmed many years ago. Sheaves of grain were tied together
and stood on end to dry.

HE'S NOT FAR FROM HOME    *1986   Acrylic on canvas   50.80 cm x 60.96 cm (20" x 24")   Allen Sapp*
Not everyone on the reserve was close to a well, so often men would have to go with their horses and
bring water home in a barrel.

LIL' FELLOW WATCHING HIS DAD    1994
*Acrylic on canvas    55.88 cm x 55.88 cm*
*(22" x 22")    Allen Sapp*
Little boys were no different when I was young
than they are today. It always felt good to be
around Dad and watch him work.

HAULING A LOAD OF WOOD HOME
*1996 Acrylic on canvas 60.96 cm x 60.96 cm
(24" x 24") Allen Sapp*
The end of a good day. Two dependable
horses, a full load of wood, and two
satisfied men heading home.

PULLING MY LIL' BROTHER    *1994*
*Acrylic on canvas    50.80 cm x 50.80 cm*
*(20" x 20")    Allen Sapp*
We would have fun with our sleds and my little
brother liked me to pull him on the sled.

GRANDFATHER'S HELPER FEEDING THE
COWS   *1996   Acrylic on canvas*
*60.96 cm x 60.96 cm (24" x 24")   Allen Sapp*
One of my grandfather's helpers looking after
the cows was Alex Nicotine, who also lived on
the Red Pheasant Reserve.

EATING BANNOCK OUTSIDE  *1995*
*Acrylic on canvas  50.80 cm x 50.80 cm*
*(20" x 20")  Allen Sapp*
Bannock was always a favourite for both young and old and would taste especially good when it was eaten outdoors beside an open fire.

PARENTS WATCHNG THEIR KIDS PLAY HOCKEY    *1995   Acrylic on canvas   60.96 cm x 91.44 cm (24" x 36")   Allen Sapp*
We would make some ice behind the house and sometimes there would be enough kids to have a game. Gramma and Grampa
would come out to watch them play.

ESQUOIO COMING FROM SEWING    *1993   Acrylic on canvas   121.92 cm x 182.88 cm (48" x 72")   Allen Sapp*

Esquoio is Cree for Indian lady. Ladies would often visit one another when they were sewing.

THEY'RE GOING TO VISIT    *1988   Acrylic on canvas   50.80 cm x 60.96 cm (20" x 24")   Allen Sapp*
People always enjoyed visiting, and as long as you had a good team of horses you could always
go anywhere in the winter.

LIL' FELLOWS PLAYING    *1990   Acrylic on canvas   40.64 cm x 50.80 cm (16" x 20")   Allen Sapp*
This painting has been chosen by UNICEF to be part of the 1996 card series, celebrating
its fiftieth anniversary.

GOING TO FEED THE HORSES    *1993   Acrylic on canvas   40.64 cm x 50.80 cm (16" x 20")   Allen Sapp*
My dad and grandfather always made sure that the horses were fed at the end of the day, and I remember
helping them as I grew up.

BRINGING A JUMPING DEER HOME    *1968   Acrylic on*
*masonite   60.96 cm x 50.80 cm (24" x 20")   Allen Sapp*
My dad was a good hunter and I would go out with him sometimes when he hunted for deer or rabbits. The deer would be
brought home and nothing was wasted.

**WAITING FOR A FRIEND**   *1974   Acrylic on canvas   45.72 cm x 60.96 cm (18" x 24")   Allen Sapp*
Time seems to stand still when you are alone with your horse waiting for a friend. The old wagon
wheel reminds us of a time when no one was in a hurry.

STARTING TO MAKE A TENT    *1970   Acrylic on canvas*
*50.80 cm x 40.64 cm (20" x 16")   Allen Sapp*
It is very important when making a tent or tipi to have straight
sticks of wood that are firm and strong.

# Index to Paintings

Height precedes width on reproductions.

# Appendix

SELECTED ONE-PERSON EXHIBITIONS

### 1968

Eaton's Art Gallery, Montreal, Quebec

Marquis Hall, University of Saskatchewan, Saskatoon, Saskatchewan

St. Thomas More College, University of Saskatchewan, Saskatoon, Saskatchewan

Teacher's College, Saskatoon, Saskatchewan

Wynona Mulcaster's home, Saskatoon, Saskatchewan

### 1969

Mendel Art Gallery, Saskatoon, Saskatchewan

Robertson Art Gallery, Ottawa, Ontario

Zachary Walter Gallery, Los Angeles, California

### 1970

Alex Fraser Galleries, Vancouver, British Columbia

Alwin Gallery, London, England

Centennial Art Gallery, Halifax, Nova Scotia

The Gainsborough Galleries, Calgary, Alberta

International Music Camp, Bottineau, North Dakota

Mendel Art Gallery, Saskatoon, Saskatchewan

Moose Jaw Art Museum, Moose Jaw, Saskatchewan

New Brunswick Museum, Saint John, New Brunswick

Saskatchewan Power Corporation Building, Regina, Saskatchewan

Upstairs Gallery, Winnipeg, Manitoba

### 1971

Alwin Gallery, London, England

Damkjar-Burton Gallery, Hamilton, Ontario

Downstairs Gallery, Edmonton, Alberta

Gallery of the Golden Key, Vancouver, British Columbia

Langara Gardens, Vancouver, British Columbia

Memorial University Art Gallery, St. John's, Newfoundland

The Print Gallery, Victoria, British Columbia

Robertson Art Gallery, Ottawa, Ontario

The Sonneck Gallery, Kitchener, Ontario

St. John's Ravenscourt School, Fort Garry, Manitoba

Zachary Walter Gallery, Los Angeles, California

### 1972

Alwin Gallery, London, England

Damkjar-Burton Gallery, Hamilton, Ontario

Downstairs Gallery, Edmonton, Alberta
Eaton's Art Gallery, Toronto, Ontario
The Gainsborough Galleries, Calgary, Alberta
Gallery of the Golden Key, Vancouver, British Columbia

1973
Downstairs Gallery, Edmonton, Alberta
Eaton's Art Gallery, Toronto, Ontario
Gallery of the Golden Key, Vancouver, British Columbia

1974
Alwin Gallery, London, England
Continental Galleries, Montreal, Quebec
de Vooght Galleries, Vancouver, British Columbia
Downstairs Gallery, Edmonton, Alberta
Zachary Walter Gallery, Los Angeles, California

1975
Eaton's Art Gallery, Toronto, Ontario
de Vooght Galleries, Vancouver, British Columbia
The Gainsborough Galleries, Calgary, Alberta

1976
de Vooght Galleries, Vancouver, British Columbia
Eaton's Art Gallery, Toronto, Ontario
Edmonton Art Mart, Edmonton, Alberta

Hammer Galleries, New York City, New York
Rowe House Gallery, Washington, D.C.

1977
Assiniboia Gallery, Regina, Saskatchewan
Continental Galleries, Montreal, Quebec
de Vooght Galleries, Vancouver, British Columbia
Edmonton Art Mart, Edmonton, Alberta
The Gainsborough Galleries, Calgary, Alberta
Mendel Art Gallery, Saskatoon, Saskatchewan
Swift Current National Exhibition Centre, Swift Current,
  Saskatchewan

1978
Assiniboia Gallery, Regina, Saskatchewan

1979
Gainsborough Galleries Ltd., Calgary, Alberta

1980
Gainsborough Galleries Ltd., Calgary, Alberta

1981
Assiniboia Gallery, Regina, Saskatchewan
Downstairs Gallery, Edmonton, Alberta
Robertson Galleries, Ottawa, Ontario

1982
Gainsborough Galleries Ltd., Calgary, Alberta

1983
Assiniboia Gallery, Regina, Saskatchewan
Downstairs Gallery, Edmonton, Alberta
Robertson Galleries, Ottawa, Ontario

1985
Assiniboia Gallery, Regina, Saskatchewan
Heffel Galleries, Vancouver, British Columbia

1986
Assiniboia Bessborough Gallery, Saskatoon, Saskatchewan
Lourie Gallery, Toronto, Ontario

1987
Hollander-York Gallery, Toronto, Ontario
Robertson Galleries, Ottawa, Ontario

1988
Agassiz Galleries, Winnipeg, Manitoba
Lourie Gallery, Toronto, Ontario

1989
Allen Sapp Gallery: The Gonor Collection, North
    Battleford, Saskatchewan

La Galerie Continentale, Montreal, Quebec
Woltjen-Udell Gallery, Edmonton, Alberta

1990
Allen Sapp Gallery: The Gonor Collection, North
    Battleford, Saskatchewan
Masters Gallery, Calgary, Alberta
The Raven Gallery, Minneapolis, Minnesota
Robertson Galleries, Ottawa, Ontario
Wilfert's Hambleton Galleries, Kelowna, British Columbia

1991
Allen Sapp Gallery: The Gonor Collection, North
    Battleford, Saskatchewan
Galerie de Bellefeuille, Montreal, Quebec
West End Gallery, Edmonton, Alberta

1992
Allen Sapp Gallery: The Gonor Collection, North
    Battleford, Saskatchewan
Assiniboia Gallery, Regina, Saskatchewan
Assiniboia Bessborough Gallery, Saskatoon,
    Saskatchewan
Clymer Art Museum & Gallery, Ellensburg, Washington
Lourie Gallery, Toronto, Ontario
Wilfert's Hambleton Galleries, Kelowna, British
    Columbia

1993

Allen Sapp Gallery: The Gonor Collection, North
    Battleford, Saskatchewan
Hollander-York Gallery, Toronto, Ontario
Humberston-Edwards Gallery, Vancouver, British
    Columbia
Masters Gallery, Calgary, Alberta
West End Gallery, Edmonton, Alberta

1994

Allen Sapp Gallery: The Gonor Collection, North
    Battleford, Saskatchewan
Assiniboia Bessborough, Saskatoon, Saskatchewan
Assiniboia Gallery, Regina, Saskatchewan
Galerie de Bellefeuille, Montreal, Quebec
Wilfert's Hambleton Galleries, Kelowna, British Columbia

1995

Galerie de Bellefeuille, Montreal, Quebec
West End Gallery, Edmonton, Alberta
Hollander-York Gallery, Toronto, Ontario
*Kiskayetum – Allen Sapp: A Retrospective*
    MacKenzie Art Gallery, Regina, Saskatchewan
    Mendel Art Gallery, Saskatoon, Saskatchewan
    Allen Sapp Gallery: The Gonor Collection, North
    Battleford, Saskatchewan

1996

Humberston-Edwards Gallery, Vancouver, British Columbia
Hambleton Galleries, Kelowna, British Columbia
Masters Gallery, Calgary, Alberta
*Kiskayetum – Allen Sapp: A Retrospective*
    Thunder Bay Art Gallery, Thunder Bay, Ontario
    Southern Alberta Art Gallery, Lethbridge, Alberta
    Canadian Museum of Civilization, Hull, Quebec

SELECTED GROUP EXHIBITIONS

1974

*Canadian Indian Art '74*, Royal Ontario Museum, Toronto, Ontario

1977

*Links to a Tradition*, organized by the Department of Indian Affairs
    and Northern Development for travel to Brazil

1982

*Tailfeathers/Sapp/Janvier: Selections from the Art Collection of the Glenbow
    Museum*, Thunder Bay Art Gallery, Thunder Bay, Ontario

1982

*Renewal*, Masterworks of Contemporary Indian Art from the
    National Museum of Man, Thunder Bay Art Gallery, Thunder
    Bay, Ontario

1983

*Contemporary Indian Art at Rideau Hall* from the permanent collection of the Department of Indian Affairs and Northern Development, Ottawa, Ontario

1983

*Contemporary Canadian Native Art*, United Nations General Assembly Building, New York City, New York

1983–1985

*Contemporary Indian and Inuit Art of Canada*, organized by the Department of Indian Affairs and Northern Development for travel to the United States and Canada

1985

*Two Worlds*, MacKenzie Art Gallery, Regina, Saskatchewan

1986

*New Beginnings*, Native Business Summit, Toronto, Ontario

1986

*A Celebration of Contemporary Canadian Native Art*, Southwest Museum, Los Angeles, California

1987

*Eight from the Prairies*, Thunder Bay Art Gallery, Thunder Bay, Ontario

1995

*Moscow Exhibition*, Ottawa, Ontario

## FILMS AND TELEVISION

1971

CBC Television. "Allen Sapp: By Instinct a Painter." *The Nature of Things*, Bill Zborowsky producer (23 Nov.).

1973

National Film Board of Canada. *Colours of Pride*, Henning Jacobsen Productions Limited for the Department of Indian Affairs and Northern Development.

1983

CBC Television. *Four Prairie Artists*, Donnalu Wigmore producer.

1989

STV Television Saskatoon. "Allen Sapp." *For Art's Sake*, Bill Morrison producer.

1994

*On the Road Again*, CBC Television Host Wayne Rostad.

SELECTED BIBLIOGRAPHY

1968

"Cree Artist Displays Artistry." *The Star Phoenix*, Saskatoon
(17 Aug.).
"Art Show Features Allen Sapp." *North Battleford News-
Optimist* (17 Sept.).

1969

Bradshaw, Thecla (Zeeh). *Recent Paintings by Allen Sapp.*
  Saskatoon: Mendel Art Gallery.
"Cree Artist's Show a Great Success." *The Indian News*,
  Ottawa, 12:8.
"Saskatchewan Indian Adept as Painter." *The Star Phoenix*,
  Saskatoon (21 March).
"Mendel Gallery Popular." *The Star Phoenix*, Saskatoon
  (8 April).
"Many Indians Found Unaware of Training Programs
  Available." *The Star Phoenix*, Saskatoon (25 April).
"A Cree Artist Hits the World Market." *Star Weekly*, Toronto
  (7 June).
Melvile, Idabelle. "Allen Sapp: Indian Artist." *Western
  Producer*, Saskatoon (10 July).

Ketchum, W. Q. "Art News and Views." *Ottawa Journal*
  (Oct.).
"Indian's Works in Ottawa Gallery." *The Star Phoenix*,
  Saskatoon (21 Oct.).
"Chrétien Praises Cree Indian Artist." *Ottawa Journal*
  (21 Oct.).
Bergin, Jenny. "Indian Paints Story of Life on a
  Reservation." *The Ottawa Citizen* (23 Oct.).
"One-Man Showing for Canada's New Discovery." *The
  Ottawa Citizen* (25 Oct.).
"Sapp Gets Indian Art Exhibit." *The Sun-Telegram*, Vancouver
  (9 Nov.).
Estebans, Jorge. "Art Matters." *The Canyon Crier*, Los
  Angeles (17 Nov.).
Pratt, Florence. "Allen Sapp's Paintings to Be Viewed in
  England." *The Star Phoenix*, Saskatoon (20 Dec.).

1970

"The World of Allen Sapp." Calgary: Gainsborough
  Galleries Limited.
Walker, Richard. "Profile of Allen Sapp." *Arts Review*,
  21:26 (Jan.).
MacEwan, J. W. Grant. "Our Natural Heritage." *Calgary
  Herald* (2 Jan.).
Thomas, Sheila. "Cree Artist on Road to Success."
  *Calgary Herald* (7 Jan.).

Thomas, Sheila. "Indian Artist Acclaimed." *Province*, Vancouver (9 Jan.).

Thomas, Sheila. "Shy, Eloquent Indian Introduces His People." *Edmonton Journal* (16 Jan.).

Thomas, Sheila. "Shy Cree Artist Paints Clear Visions of His Life, Land." *Montreal Star* (20 Jan.).

Thomas, Sheila. "Cree Indian Artist Wins International Attention in London." *The Ottawa Citizen* (24 Jan.).

Moore, Tom. "Tom Moore – Man About Town." *The Albertan*, Calgary (23 April).

"Indian Artist to Display Work." *Calgary Herald* (23 April).

van der Hoogen, Anne. "Indian Artist's Works Now on Display Here." Calgary Herald (1 May).

Hoedtke, Frank J. "Artist's Work Lauded." *Calgary Herald* (4 May).

McLean, Helen. "Art on Show Is Mixed Bag." *The Albertan*, Calgary (5 May).

Pratt, Florence. "Second Exhibition by Sapp." *The Star Phoenix*, Saskatoon (10 July).

Percival, Robert M. "Allen Sapp: Paintings." *artscanada*, nos. 148–149 (Oct./Nov.).

Kanienski, Jan. "Sapp Nostalgic, Exotic, Pokrant Shocks in Art Shows." *Winnipeg Tribune* (24 Oct.).

Peters, Mary Jane. "Allen Sapp." *Tawow: Canadian Indian Cultural Magazine*, 1:3 (Autumn/Winter).

### 1971

MacEwan, J. W. Grant. "Allen Sapp: By Instinct a Painter." *Portraits from the Plains*, Toronto/New York: McGraw-Hill Co. of Canada

Wilson, William. *Los Angeles Times* (12 Feb.).

Kennedy, Carol. "Canadian Indian's Works Snapped Up by Eager Buyers at London Gallery." *The Vancouver Sun* (1 April).

Kennedy, Carol. "Cree Art 'Hot' in London." *The Montreal Star* (1 April).

"Paintings by Saskatchewan Cree Selling Fast." *Toronto Telegram* (1 April).

"London Buying Saskatchewan Cree's Work." *The Abertan*, Calgary (2 April).

Kennedy, Carol. "London Sales Good for Sapp's Art." *The Star Phoenix*, Saskatoon (30 April).

Thomas, Bill. *Daily Colonist*, Victoria (3 Sept.).

"Artistry of Cree Indian Gets Canadian TV Exposure." *The Star Phoenix*, Saskatoon (22 Nov.).

"Story of a Cree Artist." *Dartmouth Free Press* (22 Nov.).

### 1972

Kritzwiser, Kay. "The Primitive Touch in Sapp's Acrylics." *The Globe and Mail*, Toronto (31 March).

"Prairie Paintings Get Cree Off Dole." *Vancouver Sun* (24 April).

"Cree Exhibits Work." *Edmonton Journal* (28 April).

"Indian Painter Winning Acclaim." *Montreal Star* (1 May).

"Indian Artist Special Repeated." *Calgary Herald* (5 May).

"Saskatchewan Allen Sapp Achieving Artistic Rewards." *The Star Phoenix*, Saskatoon (28 Sept.).

1973

Warner, John Anson. "The Cree Artist Allen Sapp." *The Beaver*, Winnipeg (Winter).

Cipriette, Elmo. "Saskatchewan Painter's Works Are Much in Demand." *The Leader-Post*, Regina (13 Nov.).

"His Paintings Sell So Fast, He Has Few Left in Reserve." *Calgary Herald* (15 Nov.).

1974

Nordstrom, Inez B. "Profile of Cree Artist, Allen Sapp." *The North Battleford News-Optimist* (4 Oct.).

Kosinski, Marytka L. "The Art of a Simple Honest Man." *Edmonton Journal* (20 Nov.).

1975

Warner, John Anson. "The Cree Artist Allen Sapp." *The Beaver*, Winnipeg (Summer).

Lovoos, Janice. "Allen Sapp, Cree Indian Artist." *Southwest Art* (Jan.).

McIntosh, Irwin. "The Making of a Great Artist." *North Battleford News-Optimist* (28 Nov.).

"Well-Known Indian Artist Elected to RCA." *The Saskatchewan Indian* (Dec.).

1976

Hammer, Victor. *Allen Sapp: By Instinct a Painter*. New York: Hammer Galleries.

"Arts Academy Honours N.B. Resident." *The Star Phoenix*, Saskatoon (12 Jan.).

*North Battleford News-Optimist* (13 Jan.).

Loercher, Diana. "A Uniquely Indian Vision – In Manhattan." *Christian Science Monitor* (5 May).

MacGregor, Ron. "Home-Grown Talent." *Edmonton Journal* (15 May).

*North Battleford News-Optimist* (21 Sept.).

Warner, John Anson. "Allen Sapp, Cree Painter." *American Indian Art*, 2:1 (1 Nov.).

"Visiting Brother at Red Pheasant Reserve." *Indian Arts Calendar* (Dec.).

1977

Warner, John Anson and Bradshaw, Thecla. *A Cree Life: The Art of Allen Sapp*. Vancouver: J. J. Douglas Ltd.

Warner, John Anson. "The Art of Allen Sapp: A Study in the Sociology of Art." Presentation at the Annual Meeting of the Canadian Sociology and Anthropology Association (CSAA), Fredericton, New Brunswick (10–13 June).

Edmonstone, Wayne. "The Magic World of Allen Sapp." *Vancouver Sun* (4 Nov.).

Earl, Marjorie. "Wonders of the Prairies Haunt Allen Sapp Art Book." *Winnipeg Tribune* (8 Nov.).

Watmough, David. "On the Coffee Table It's Sapp Over Thomson." *Metro Magazine*, Toronto (10 Nov.).

Russell, Nancy. "Sapp's Character Still Mystery." *The Star Phoenix*, Saskatoon (12 Nov.).

Fenton, Terry. "For the Record." *Edmonton Journal* (28 Nov.).

Warwick, Susan. "Allen Sapp Signs Books." *The North Battleford Advertiser Post* (30 Nov.).

Hladun, Helene. "An Artist's Painted Memories of Indian Life." *The Albertan*, Calgary (17 Dec.).

Cuthbertson, Ken.  "Allen Sapp Has Earned the Respect of Both Cultures." *The Leader-Post*, Regina (20 Dec.).

"A Cree Life." *The Star*, Toronto (24 Dec.).


1978

"Allen Sapp, by Instinct a Painter." *The Native Perspective*, 3:2.

Rolfe, Elaine. "Works of Canadian Painters Line the Committee Rooms at Canadian Medical Association's House." *Canadian Medical Association Journal*, 118:4 (18 Feb.).

"Gallery for Determined Artists." *San Diego Union* (21 May).

1979

Warner, John Anson. "Visual Arts: Allen Sapp." *Artswest* (Sept./Oct.).

MacEwan, J. W. Grant. "Indian Artist One of Canada's Foremost Success Stories." *Calgary Herald* (6 Oct.).

Burt, Eric O. "Card Features Allen Sapp Painting." *The Star Phoenix*, Saskatoon (20 Oct.).

Percival, Robert M. "Allen Sapp: Paintings." *artscanada*, nos. 148–149 (Oct./Nov.).


1980

Highwater, Jamake. *The Sweetgrass Lives On: Fifty Contemporary North American Indian Artists*. New York: Lippincott & Crowell Publishing.

Cochran, Bente Roed, *Edmonton Journal* (22 April).


1982

McLuhan, Elizabeth. *Tailfeathers/Sapp/Janvier: Selections from the Art Collection of the Glenbow Museum*. Thunder Bay: Thunder Bay Art Gallery.

"Portraits of His People." *Skyword*, Pacific Western Airlines Inflight Magazine (March).


1983

Leeper, Muriel.  "Allen Sapp: Scenes From Childhood Through Allen Sapp's Art." *Prairie Arts*, 1:3 (Feb.).

Bellegarde, William. "World Famous." *AMMSA* (18 March).

Baile, Nancy. *The Ottawa Citizen* (9 April).

Wurts, Rosemary. "Painter Allen Sapp: Eloquent in His Art." *Western People* (23 June).

"Northern Impressions." *Skyword*, Pacific Western Airlines Inflight Magazine (Oct.).

**1984**

Rees, Ronald. *Land of Earth and Sky: Landscape Painting of Western Canada*. Saskatoon: Western Producer Prairie Books.

Warner, John Anson. "Contemporary Canadian Indian Art." *Anthropology of The Americas Masterkey*, Los Angeles: Southwest Museum.

Ball, Denise. "New Gallery is Devoted to Promotion of Native Artist." *The Leader-Post*, Regina (20 Sept.).

**1985**

*Two Worlds*. Regina: Norman MacKenzie Art Gallery.

Robertson, Sheila. "Indian Art Traverses Time, Space." *The Star Phoenix*, Saskatoon (22 June).

Hesse, Jayne. "A Point of Pride." *Battleford Telegraph*, (2 Oct.).

Perry, Meta. "Regina Exhibition Shows Changes in Acclaimed Artist Sapp." *The Leader-Post*, Regina (14 Nov.).

*Canadian Encyclopedia*. Edmonton: Hurtig, vol. 3, 1634.

**1987**

Podedworny, Carol. *Eight from the Prairies*. Thunder Bay: Thunder Bay Art Gallery.

"Saskatchewan Residents Honored." *The Star Phoenix*, Saskatoon (17 Jan.).

MacDonald, Heather. "Sapp Art Collection Transferring to New Site." *The Star Phoenix*, Saskatoon (9 Nov.).

**1988**

Boxall, Michael. "Allen Sapp Gallery." *Western Living*, Saskatoon/Calgary (Dec.).

**1989**

Bauche, D. G. *"Naheyow": A Portrait of Allen Sapp and His People*. North Battleford: The Allen Sapp Gallery – The Gonor Collection.

Robertson, Sheila. "Sapp Sees Art As Reflection of Cree Life for Posterity." *The Star Phoenix*, Saskatoon (24 Jan.).

Einsiedler, Owen. "Battleford's Gallery to Preserve Works." *The Star Phoenix*, Saskatoon (28 Jan.).

Robertson, Sheila. "Allen Sapp Celebrated As Hero in North Battleford." *The Star Phoenix*, Saskatoon (6 May).

"Cree Artist's Work Finds a Home." *Edmonton Journal* (8 May).

"A Remarkable Tribute to a Special Artist." *Saskatchewan Report* (Sept.).

Bergan, Chan. "Gallery." *Western Horseman* (Oct.).

MacDonald, Max. "Home Town Recognition Touches Artist's Heart." *The Leader-Post*, Regina (25 Nov.).

MacDonald, Max. "A City Pays Tribute to Its Artist Son: Allen Sapp." *The Star Phoenix*, Saskatoon (23 Dec.).

1990

Kinsella, W. P. *Two Spirits Soar: The Art of Allen Sapp*. Toronto: Stoddart Publishing Co. Limited.

Wagamese, Richard. "Paintings Reveal the Real Story: Kinsella Can't Match the Power of Sapp's Legacy." *Calgary Herald* (6 Feb.).

MacDonald, Max. "Chronicler of the Cree." *Canadian Geographic* (Aug./Sept.).

MacDonald, Max. "Bond Between Artist and Patron." *The Star Phoenix*, Saskatoon (1 Dec.).

1991

Murray, Maureen. "A Window to the Past." *Epic* (July).

1992

*Saskatchewan Report* (Feb.).

"UNICEF Tribute for Indian's Art." *Prince Albert Herald* (5 May).

"Sapp Hasn't Forgotten His Roots." *The Leader-Post*, Regina (6 Oct.).

1993

"SIFC *Powwow Times* Cover Contributed by Allen Sapp." SIFC *Powwow Times* (April).

## ALLEN SAPP AND UNICEF

Allen Sapp's life-long love for children and his desire to help raise money for children all over the world was recognized and rewarded when his donation to UNICEF's greeting card programme of an original work entitled "Christmas Evening" was featured on one of the top-selling UNICEF greeting cards in 1979, The International Year of the Child. In 1986 Allen Sapp's painting "Puppies" was selected for a UNICEF greeting card. Allen Sapp was again requested to participate in the selection for 1996 and three of his images have been chosen:

"Nokum Coming To Visit"
"Lil' Fellows Playing"
"Two Lil' Kids Sliding."

UNICEF is the only organization within the United Nations system dedicated exclusively to the welfare of children. Since 1950 UNICEF has reproduced artwork on greeting cards as a means to promote its program, to raise funds for UNICEF-assisted projects, and to increase awareness of its concerns for children worldwide. Since that time, thousands of artists, representing over 140 countries, have donated the right to reproduce their works. UNICEF cards are renowned throughout the world for their beauty and for the good work they support.

UNICEF's selection process for greeting card designs is a careful one. Art experts, representatives of UNICEF's National Committees and marketing specialists decide on the works of art submitted to the International Image Selection Committee. In 1995 the selection for the 50th Anniversary 1996 Greeting Card collection was made at the International Greeting Card Workshop for National Committees.

On behalf of the world's children, UNICEF extends its heartfelt appreciation to Allen Sapp for his generous support. We are particularly grateful that the money raised from the sale of his greeting cards and from the sale of his original works of art depicting the greeting card scenes will generate a tremendous amount of revenue to help provide health care, nutrition, education, and safe drinking water to the world's children.

ALLEN SAPP'S DEALERS

For almost thirty years, Allen Sapp has exhibited with numerous galleries across Canada, the United States, and Europe. These exhibitions have brought the paintings of Allen Sapp into the lives of thousands of admirers and collectors. The works of Allen Sapp may be found at the following commercial galleries in Canada.

Assiniboia Gallery, Regina, Saskatchewan
Assiniboia Bessborough Gallery, Saskatoon, Saskatchewan
Canada House, Banff, Alberta
Galerie de Bellefeuille, Montreal, Quebec
Hambleton Galleries, Kelowna, British Columbia
Hollander-York Gallery, Toronto, Ontario

Humberston Edwards Fine Art, West Vancouver, British Columbia
Loch Mayberry Fine Art, Winnipeg, Manitoba
Masters Gallery Ltd., Calgary, Alberta
Robertson Galleries, Ottawa, Ontario
West End Gallery, Edmonton, Alberta
West End Gallery, Victoria, British Columbia

Allen Sapp Paintings Inc. 2429 - 11th Avenue, Regina, Saskatchewan S4P 0K4
Allen Sapp Gallery – The Gonor Collection 1091 - 100th Street, North Battleford, Saskatchewan S9A 0V2